Poems, Prose, and Verse

Compiled by
Adele Handfield,
Founder of *The Lamp Post*

For all submitters of
The Lamp Post

Copyright © 2022 by Adele Handfield
Text copyright © 2022 by Adele Handfield, Eleanor Handfield, Nora Sauder, Lillian Cawood, Emma Cawood, Selah Cross, Kami Hatton, Hudson Hatton, Amanda Crooker, Caleb Crooker, Kailyn Kott
Illustrations copyright © 2022 by Adele Handfield, Nora Sauder, Emma Cawood, Sparrow Wester, Autumn Slatcha, Libby Cross

All rights reserved.
No part of this book may be duplicated in any manner whatsoever without the express written consent of the publisher, except in the form of brief excerpts of quotations used for the purposes of review. To make an inquiry about duplication etc., contact the publisher at tlpnewsless.blogspot.com.

Names: Handfield, Adele — author | Handfield, Adele — illustrator | Sauder, Nora — author | Sauder, Nora — illustrator | Cawood, Emma — illustrator | Wester, Sparrow — illustrator | Cawood, Lillian — author | Cross, Libby — illustrator | Cross, Selah — illustrator | Hatton, Kami — author | Hatton, Hudson — author | Crooker, Amanda — author | Crooker, Caleb — author | Slatcha, Autumn — illustrator | Kott, Kailyn — author
Title: Poems, prose, and verse / Adele Handfield
Fonts: display: Belights. Serif: Cochin.

Identifiers: ISBN: 978-1-4357-8897-8 (paperback)
Imprint: lulu.com
Subjects: Poetry—Children's | Art—Poetry
Printed in the U.S.A.

Published by *The Lamp Post Library*.

Yellow Flower
by Adele Handfield

Table of Contents

Summer into Autumn	6
Winter	8
Snow, Like Whispers	10
A Rainy Day	12
The First Snow	13
The Flower	16
Green Sand	18
How Jane Escaped	20
I wish	22
A Faerie's House Is In A Cloude	24
Pure with Perfection	26
The Acadie	27
Splash	29
In Battle with Jeanne D'Puchelle	31
Grammatical Poem	32
The Moment Between	34
Sunset and Moonrise	34
Grass	36
Mixing Frosting	38
The Field of Flowers	40
Adele Handfield	42

Eleanor Handfield	43
Lillian Cawood	44
Emma Cawood	45
Sparrow Wester	46
Trace Wester	47
Libby Cross	48
Selah Cross	49
Autumn Slatcha	50
Kami & Hudson Hatton	51
Amanda Crooker	52
Caleb Crooker	53
Nora Sauder	54
Kailyn Kott	55

Summer into Autumn

By Adele Handfield, 13

—

Summer into autumn
Is a wonderful time,
In which cool breezes blow.
The rushing streams are still warm,
Still warm from the summer sun.
A few early trees have turned
Glimpses of red and gold.
The air is perfect, with a touch of cool,
And the birds are still chirping,
They are chirping and singing, happily.

Flower Bouquet
By Eleanor Handfield

Winter

By Adele Handfield, 13

Winter is the season,
Of white, white snow.
White, powdery, pure,
Snowflakes, lighting on your mitten,
And lighting on the ground.
And tall, strong evergreens,
Needled, snowy-laden.
Snowdrops and fiddlehead ferns
End this magical time
Which some detest,
And some love.
I am of the latter.

The Gift
by Adele Handfield

Snow, Like Whispers

By Adele Handfield, 13

—

Last time then was cold
And icy winds had taken hold,
Of the breeze-blown colour
Of oak and maple others annually,

They had since gone,
Falling off, and going brown.
This is the time of year
That no one really likes

Dirty brown leaves,
Crunching, crispy, constantly —
It comes with a cold breath,
And ice, dripping down.

It changes when the sweep of clouds
Bring down other than ice and rain
Bringing down soft cold whispers,
Cooling, though no pain.

Soft, sweet, tasteless fluffiness
Fluffing on my hair,
My scarf and eyelashes catching them,
And when then out my tongue I bring,

It catches them, so then I sing.
Delicious, soft, fluttering flutters,

Changing the atmosphere of here,
Covering with a pure, crisp blanket,

Nature's memory foam.

Snowy, snowy, oh so light
Softly making night
Ever so soft and bright.

Guy on a Horse
By Trace Wester

A Rainy Day

By Eleanor Handfield, 7

—

Once upon a rainy day
I was riding my scooter
When it started to rain.
So I ran inside,
Where it was warm,
I stayed awhile,
And saw a movie.

The First Snow

By Lillian Cawood, 13
—

Floating and dancing oh so high,
Calling back to the dark night sky.
Not here, 'nor there, yet everywhere,
Miniature stars cling to my hair.

Softened and cold from countless flights,
Cut from the clouds of starry nights.
Clothing the trees with bright white cloaks
The cedars and the mighty oaks

Bow their branches to winter's king
Waiting for the warmth of Spring.
For even while snowflakes fall,
Days of warmer clime will call.

Song
by Libby Cross

Lilac Hydrangea
by Adele Handfield

The Flower

By Adele Handfield, 13

—

In the spring, in the green,
The cutting winds
 Are first mean

Then the chill
Leaves and now comes
A shower

Warm and sweet
Waking up the
Frozen soil.

The seeds below
Poke their heads
From the dank and deep

Sprouting slowly
Cotyledons come
And new stems arise

Petals enclosed
In soft and green
The bud is small

Yet what's inside
Is loved far and wide
And everywhere.

Opening slowly
Without a sound
Comes out a pink

Majestic cluster
Of petals.
Pink and red.

They open in
The morning light
The sun overhead

Welcoming this new
Little one.
Spreading out

Fully beautiful
This flower
In a garden

With flowers similar
But none are quite the same.
With careful watering and love

The flower grows
Tall and strong
Until one day

It is plucked away
Into a vase,
And a flower bouquet.

Green Sand

By Adele Handfield, 13

Far, far, far away,
Beyond the sandy land
It is called there, East Sand,

There is a rich forest
A deep, green, rich forest
It spreads o'er the West,

And on the other side,
East Sand is in the East.
Some say it is of least

But others will sport out
Arguments - Yes, yes! No!
Green? Sand? Where shall we go?

Perhaps one will save us
From this great misery
And simply say, "Both, we!"

The forest is green, lit,
And East Sand has soft sand
Both true, a gentle hand

Those in the Sand City,
The City of the Sand,
Think that theirs is the Land.

Those in the forest green,
In with all the wood-birds
Think that they're only to be!

Jane's House
by Adele Handfield

How Jane Escaped

By Adele Handfield, 13

—

Jane got a book
And in it she wrote
Her plans for escape in the future.
If a dragon or tiger
After her ran,
She would escape.
Through the window!
She wrote.
And if a kidnapper spotted her,
Jumping out the window,
She would escape.
Climb a tree!
She wrote.
But if a fire-breathing,
Very evil bird,
Then spotted her,
Climbing *his* tree,
She would escape.
Swing out by way of the trapeze!
She wrote.
But if her brother, Ben, was there,
Already on the trapeze,
They both would escape,
Run into the house,
And lock the door,
And run into their mother's arms.

(This drawing was submitted for the TLP cover contest Spring 2022 and won 1st place)
By Emma Cawood

By Nora Sauder
—
I wish I were a Beech Tree,
To see what I could see.
I wish I were a Willow Tree,
So I could sway with the wind as it came.

But I'd rather be me, nothing but me.
Swinging on a swing
In spring, with you!

Girls on a Swing
by Nora Sauder

A Faerie's House Is In A Cloude

By Adele Handfield, 13
—
There is something that, no,
Not everyone can now know.
      But I know.
It is where a Faerie lives —
Have you seen their small abodes?
      I've seen them.
A Faerie's house? Yes, I know.
Their houses are in the cloudes
      That I know.
There is a Faerie that I know
By the name of Linnetto,
      Her, I know.
She showed me her house — A cloude!
Many lovely rooms were there,
      That I saw.
So now I know where Faeries live
(In a white, fluffy cloude abode)
      So *I* know.
That wonder has now left my mind
With the knowledge that I bear —
      Cloude Abode!
You should have seen the gold sun
Streaming through the soft white cloude
      Streaming gold.
The sweet perfume of a cloude
There's never been a sweeter smell
      Cloude perfume.
The beds were soft and air warm
The food of marvelous taste
      De-li-cios!

Her Faerie friends gather there
Each and every dinner meal
        Faerie friends.
Shrilly laughs and happy cheer —
A Faerie's love is always near
        Happy sounds.
When I left their happy spot
I was so sad to leave them
        But I left.
Back at home, I told my tale
And then, a friend said — "I know!
        Let's all go!"
So off we went, all us friends,
Up the raenbow to the cloude
        Where they live.

Pure with Perfection

By Adele Handfield, 13

Simply, softly, true to his words,
Coming kindly, quiet like birds.

Swiftly, smoothly, loving, and sweet,
A person that is good to meet!

A voice that's silv'ry, like honey,
Perfect, pure, for you and me.

A person of your sweetest dreams?
And for you, who on him leans?

He's Jesus! The Saviour of this world,
For you, for me, the young and old!

The Acadie

By Adele Handfield, 13

—

Sadly country men and girls,
While gladly soldiers smiled,
Boarded their ships, and bringing
Their few little things.
Children crying, children working,
Aboard their ship of fate.
Silent tears or loud wild ones
All of them have some.
Softly now a child asks: "Where shall we now go?"
The mother sobs, "I do not know —
But if need go far and wide,
Wherever a welcoming place.

The dripping anchor rises from the cold bone sea,
The wind goes whipping and the ripped sails fill.
Off, to another place —
A place more welcoming.

The Lamppost
by Autumn Slatcha

Splash

By Adele Handfield, 13

The bright cool water that softly cheers,
Deep and sweet, up to their ears.
Happy children in it play,
Through the morning, and the day.

Clear, cool, where fishies swim,
Baby fish swim around him.
Splishing, splashing, cool and wet
It's the best of friends they've ever met.

Sun Soldier
By Sparrow Wester

In Battle with Jeanne D'Puchelle

By Kailyn Kott

—

Piper, play your fife before us
Onward rides the Maid and towards us
English foemen raise the chorus
Shouts and yells and onward for us
    Waves Jeanne's banner, onward charge!

Diving in the midst of battle,
"Come", she cries, "And show your mettle",
Down we drive and out like cattle
Run the English with a brattle
    Waves Jeanne's banner, onward charge!

Fifer, raise your song and shrilling
Rise the cries of preybirds wheeling
O'er the battle, Maiden reeling
On her horse, still fierce and rearing
    Waves Jeanne's banner, onward charge!

Grammatical Poem

By Adele Handfield, 13

Tomorrow is soon,
Now see the moon.
Come away,
Day after day,
Seldom have you
Done your do!
Lately, too.

Shortly after twelve had struck,
We were truly in the muck.
Here and there,
It was everywhere.
It's very true,
That the sky is blue,
But, so are you.

Yesterday was exceedingly
Good, and cruelly
Comes today. I wish
Nearly everyday I could fish.

Moon Soldier
By Sparrow Wester

The Moment Between Sunset and Moonrise

By Selah Cross, 12

The day descends.
The world is stained with golden light
 like paint running down a wet page.
The motes of light through the trees
 are like spears.
The laughing leaves are gilded with magic light.
The asters turn to amethysts,
the sunflowers to gold.
The earth is a painting,
A vast masterpiece wrought by a Great Artist.
A warm golden haze invades,
Like fairy dust falling fast and thick.
The clouds have become portals into other worlds in the unending sky.
The sun sinks through them,
like a king,
retiring to his royal bedchamber.
These moments are fleeting,
like the moon shining through a break of heavy cloud cover,
Fraught with unearthly magic.
And then the day exhales,
And the first star appears like the prick of a silver needle,
pulling the thread of night through behind it.

Future Car
by Trace Wester

Grass

By Caleb Crooker, 12

—

I like grass.
And it's nice.
Grass is very nice.
I like to look at it.
And when it turns
bright green,
you can eat
the bright green
stuff.
And it's nice
to paint.
And it's nice
to draw, too.
I like to
look and look.
And look.
And when I'm
looking at it,
I'm going
to paint it,
And I like
to pick the
seeds.
They are so
funny.
I like to pop
them in my hand.

Prancing Horse
By Trace Wester

Mixing Frosting

By Amanda Crooker

—

Paddles of metal
Curved identical to its mate

How fast can you twirl
Its puppeteer demands

Chained by solid, unforgiving metal
To its captor, who slowly, gently

Stops: the sweet torture of dance.

Mouths glide over them, unhesitating
Erasing every evidence of punishment.

Jungle gym for the tongue.

TLP Logo
By Adele Handfield

The Field of Flowers

by Kami Hatton, 8, and Hudson Hatton, 6

Today we smell the smell of spring,
And see the beautiful flowers;
And the forest buds all around,
And we run in the wavy meadow.

There are big beds of daffodils .
We run between their flowers,
And see their beauty all around
It is cold & crips and sweet.

It has been a perfect time
In the land of flowers today,
And now we go home to play!

Poetry Authors & Illustrators

Adele Handfield

Is 13, lives in New Hampshire, and is the creator of The Lamp Post, a collaborative paper founded in New Hampshire. As you can see, she writes poems, but mainly writes novels. Besides just writing, she also put many drawings in this book.

Her poems are:
Summer into Autumn
Winter
Snow, Like Whispers
The Flower
Green Sand
How Jane Escaped
A Faerie's House is in a Cloude
Pure with Perfection
The Acadie
Splash
Grammatical Poem

Her illustrations are:
Yellow Flower
The Gift
Lilac Hydrangea
Jane's House
The purple flower on the front page
And the TLP Logo!

Eleanor Handfield

Is eight, lives in New Hampshire, and often puts her work in The Lamp Post, including her "poetrie" here. She also made an illustration.

Her poem is:
A Rainy Day

Her illustration is:
Flower Bouquet

Lillian Cawood

Is 13, lives in Pennsylvania, and was born in Alabama and has since lived in Alaska, Georgia, and most recently Ontario, Canada. She enjoys writing, reading (J. R. R. Tolkien, C. S. Lewis and Patricia St. John are some of her favourite authors), and baking.

Her poem is:
The First Snow

Emma Cawood

Is 16, lives in Pennsylvania, and is an avid artist, (her favourite medium is watercolor), Shakespeare reader and skier. Her least favorite subject is math and she has an obsession with dark chocolate and coffee.

Her illustration is:
The flower contest entry

Sparrow Wester

Is 15, and lives in New Hampshire.
Some of his favourite things to do are:
Building with legos, Boffer battling, doing art, and riding bikes.
And his favourite authors are: J.R.R. Tolkien, C.S. Lewis,
and G.K. Chesterton.

His illustrations are:
Sun Soldier
Moon Soldier
He designed both of them.

Trace Wester

Is 10, lives in New Hampshire, and loves drawing, horses, and spending time with friends. He also loves acting out Shakespeare plays with his friends (see above picture).

His illustrations are:
Guy on a Horse
Prancing Horse

Libby Cross

Is 10, and lives in Maryland with her parents and four siblings. She does not like being cold or going to the dentist. She loves drawing, sweets and treats, and holding her baby brother.

Her illustration is:
Song

Selah Cross

Is 12, lives on a farmette in Maryland with her parents, four younger siblings, and a barnyard full of chickens, goats, and a donkey. When she's not in the barn, you can find her with her nose in a book or a pencil in her hand!

Her poem is:
The Moment between Sunset and Sunrise

Autumn Slatcha

Is 13, lives in Delaware, and loves reading, writing, music, and animals. She also likes baking, embroidering, and listening to audio dramas.

Her illustration is:
The Lamppost

Kami & Hudson Hatton

Kami, 8, likes to play with her brothers, she has five of them. She likes to try new things, she can be silly and creative but it usually calm and quiet and appreciates visits with her talkative friends.

Hudson, 6, likes to do flips on the trampoline and very fast jumps with his jump rope. He is often found playing with one of his siblings. He loves it when he gets to lay around listening to his favorite audiobooks.

Their poem is:
The Field of Flowers

Amanda Crooker

lives in California with her family and enjoys learning alongside her children in their Charlotte Mason homeschool.

Her poem is:
Mixing Frosting
She wrote it when she was 15.

Caleb Crooker

Is 12, lives in California, and enjoys being outside, gardening and taking care of animals. He also loves Star Wars and Lord of The Rings.

His poem is:
Grass

Wrote the poem "I wish" for the second instalment of
The Lamp Post.

Her poem is:
I wish

Her illustration is:
Girls on a Swing

Is 16, and lives in the woods of New Hampshire. She loves reading, writing, playing the piano, talking to her sister, and sports. One of her favorite things in the world is a well told story, in any form. She is currently writing two books.

Her poem is:
In Battle with Jeanne D'Puchelle

Ingram Content Group UK Ltd.
Milton Keynes UK
UKHW050621110723
424846UK00026B/34